BAD BISCUITS AND UGLY WOMEN
A Roundup of Stories

by

Liz Kingston Bettle

DORRANCE PUBLISHING CO., INC.
PITTSBURGH, PENNSYLVANIA 15222

This book is fondly dedicated to:
Andrew, who prompted me to write down all the stories,
Carolyn, who gave the book its title.

All Rights Reserved
Copyright © 2009 by Liz Kingston Bettle
No part of this book may be reproduced or transmitted in any form or by any means, electronic or mechanical, including photocopying, recording, or by any information storage and retrieval system without permission in writing from the publisher.

ISBN: 978-1-4349-0263-4

Printed in the United States of America

First Printing

For more information or to order additional books, please contract:
Dorrance Publishing Co., Inc.
701 Smithfield Street
Pittsburgh, Pennsylvania 15222
U.S.A.
1-800-788-7654
www.dorrancebookstore.com

Acknowledgements

There are enough who have expressed enthusiasm and helpful advice for this project that I have threatened to write a second book on the subject of getting the first one done!

My thanks to my mother, Cecil Kingston, who reminded me of some of the stories and some of the details. Dick, my husband, was a major help in checking spelling, proofreading, and doing the computer work to get the manuscript completed. Hal Haralson, who recently had his first book published, passed along helpful information. Early on in this process, the Reverend George Cladis read several of the stories and encouraged me to go full speed ahead. Provided I had not revealed anything unseemly, aunts, uncles, and cousins gave enthusiastic support to my journalistic endeavors. A gentleman in our church group, Clifford Wooten, stated that he thought the book was a noteworthy concept as it came as an expression of natural wit.

Certainly, I have not named everyone, but there has been, and continues to be, a wealth of friends and acquaintances who have voiced interest. I extend my thanks to them.

Introduction

Now my daddy, the late Duncan Kingston, said he never met up with either a bad biscuit or an ugly woman. No matter what the problem might be with a biscuit that had been deemed by others as "bad," he thought surely it could be salvaged. If it was burned, scrape some of the dark area off; if it was hard and dried out, split it, butter it lavishly, and toast it; if it was bitter from too much baking powder, put on enough jelly or sorghum syrup to cover up the taste; if the poor biscuit was crumbly from being made with too much shortening, go ahead and crumble it up, pour a spoonful of gravy over it, and eat it up; and finally, if the biscuit was a briquette, you could always throw it at wayward cows that got in the yard!

As for the ugly women part, Daddy insisted the "ugly" had to do with looks, not behavior. He believed each woman had some redeeming feature: nice eyes, a pretty smile, shapely legs, gorgeous hair color, delicate hands, or smooth skin, but at least something! He also held the view that "help" was readily available and should be used, if needed: hair color products, lotions, lipstick, mascara, deodorants, and of course, a good girdle.

This book is not a family history. Neither is it a chronological listing of incidents. There is little likelihood that it would ever be put in the category of a documentary. These stories have been written to preserve them and pass them along to family members, friends, and any others who would enjoy some musings from an unusual family.

Every book has to have a title, so I chose one of my daddy's sayings. He rarely said it without going into lengthy explanations about what he meant. He felt that if he did not expostulate on the statement, an unenlightened listener might go on thinking that surely there were a few ugly women in this world and a variety of bad biscuits.

Sounds Right to Me

For a year or two, it was necessary for us to live with my Kingston grandparents until we found suitable caretakers for two elderly people who very much wanted to remain in their farm house just west of Toyahvale.

I know it is not polite to eavesdrop, but as a child, I used to love to do just that. My grandparents were married for seventy-one years before either of them died. To my way of thinking (I was ten at the time), they had really interesting bedtime conversations on almost a nightly basis. On this night, as usual, the two of them went to bed when it got dark. I put on my nightie, picked up my blanket, and sneaked into the living room—all set to hear what this particular night's "offering" might be. I did not have long to wait: my grandmother began with a question:

"Will, why did I marry you instead of Will Casey? He was better looking than you and he, for sure, had more money than you."

"Well, Momma, I don't rightly know, but I figure it this way: Will Casey's dead now and I'm still around."

"Thank you, Will. I see that I made the right choice."

Whose is Whose?

My brother was nearly four years younger than I, and I was not above exploiting his youth and naiveté when we were children. The issue this time was Cracker Jacks, or more specifically, the prize inside said box of treats. We each were given our box of Cracker Jacks. I looked for the end of the box marked "prize" and quickly tore it open and seized the prize. However, I was not happy with it, so I proclaimed to my brother, while exchanging his yet unopened box for mine, "Oh honey, I'm so sorry; I got your prize by mistake."

THE RIGORS OF PUBLIC SCHOOL

I was being home-schooled out at the ranch because we were so far from town that the buses couldn't run that distance for one pupil, so I loved it when I was able to go stay with one of my in-town friends. That meant I could go to school for a day and do a great deal of socializing. One particular visit to public school first grade did not go so well. In fact, my activities on that occasion were to be an embarrassment to my mother for years to come.

The first grade teacher was Mrs. Mary Helen Pax. It was her second year to teach in Balmorhea. She and her husband had no children, and Mrs. Pax was the pianist at the local Baptist Church. While not holier-than-thou, she was most certainly a model of social decorum and upright behavior. Everyone in the small town well knew Mrs. Pax's upstanding reputation.

My friend Carolyn, whom I had come to town to visit, thought she was doing Mrs. Pax and the class a real favor. She announced, "Mrs. Pax, Lizzie knows a poem and can say it for us."

And thus I proceeded to get up in front of all present, and repeat, without hesitation, "Alkali Ike's Zippers":

> Now speakin' of zippers, sez Alkali Ike,
> them zippers is somethin' I really don't like.
> I aimed to buy clothes like I always had wore 'til I got to
> lookin' around in the store. They had some new shirts and
> overalls that fastened with zippers; no buttons at all.
> 'Cause where there's alkali water to drink,
> things can happen sooner than what you might think.
> So I got me some clothes that was rigged up like that and took
> them back to my camp on the alkali flat. The next mornin' I'd
> traveled for maybe a mile when the time came to give them new
> zippers a trial.
> I grab at the handle and give 'em a jerk,
> but Holy O Golden them zippers don't work! I fuss and I
> fret. I am sure out of luck,
> I started 'er crooked; the zipper is stuck.
> I swear & I sweat 'til I get the thing straight...then the

zipper it works, but a little too late!
So the next thing I do is to throw them new garments up into a
cactus for ants and for varmints,
and I reckon that buttons is safer at that
for us fellers that live on the Alkali Flats!

Ah, as the other members of the congregation listened attentively to Mrs. Pax playing the strains of "Amazing Grace," always tripping through the back of my mother's mind was "Now speakin' of zippers...."

How High the Water?

The five Kingston siblings, four boys and one girl, were well known for loud voices and argumentative natures. On this particular occasion, Uncle Joe and Daddy were going to decide about building a watering trough at the lower crossing windmill. They met at the appointed time and place, each armed with his personal ideas about specifications for the proposed trough. Guess what? The two men did not agree!

The major point of contention was the height (depth) of the trough and how it could best accommodate the cattle that would come there to drink. As they bantered back and forth, neither conceding nor compromising, Uncle Joe dropped down on his hands and knees to prove by demonstration exactly how high the trough needed to be. About that time, Mr. Cox, the government trapper, came along. When he witnessed the action from afar, he quickly wheeled to a stop and jumped out of his vehicle because he feared something unfortunate might have happened to Uncle Joe. Uncle Joe stood up and assured Mr. Cox that there was no problem, just a disagreement about how to build a water trough! None of us ever knew which man's plan was used, but the trough was built, the cattle had water, and Mr. Cox told us his account of it all.

THAT GOOD RANCH WATER

From time to time, Fred Stroade, a local farmer and trucker, would call Daddy to make a run to San Angelo or Fort Worth with him. It was a long and lonely haul, and Fred enjoyed the company. One day Fred met Daddy in town and said, "Say, Dunc, I've gotta go to Fort Worth later today. Do you wanna go with me?"

Daddy agreed, with one provision: he had to go to the ranch (eighteen miles away) first and get his can of drinking water. Fred agreed to wait as he well knew Duncan Kingston's "thing" about having that good, fresh, spring water from the ranch to drink. The water can was procured, and the two men headed east in the eighteen-wheeler. At suppertime, they pulled into a roadside diner to get something to eat. Daddy took his two-gallon can of ranch water in to get a little ice put in before they left the diner. The waitress took their orders and brought their food. Dad asked if he could get a little ice for his water can.

"Sure," she said. She took the can to the back. When she returned, she explained, "Sir, not only did I put ice in it, but also I dumped out the old water and put in some fresh."

My daddy did not leave that waitress a tip!

YOUR SISTER IS SHY, ISN'T SHE?

My husband, our (adopted) children, and I were living at Havelock, North Carolina, at the time. We had ventured over to Jacksonville one Saturday. Anna, our Chinese daughter, was five, and Andrew, our mixed-race son, was three, so when lunch time came, they were eager to go to their favorite fast-food place to eat. We sat in a booth just across from two older ladies. It did not take long for the two of them to strike up a conversation with the children. As usual, Andrew (the "mouth of the South") was doing the talking. After several minutes of questions and answers, one of the ladies said to Andrew, "Your sister is shy, isn't she?"

"Oh no," replied Andrew, "she's Chinese."

We all laughed, Anna still didn't have much to say, and we continued to enjoy our burgers!

Big Boy and the Apple Pie

Years ago, dinner-on-the-grounds at church was a major event. The noon meal after the morning service was always well attended. Each lady of the congregation eagerly brought her best dish to showcase at these occasions. My maternal grandfather, Claud Dean, was a growing boy, observing all the food as it was put out on the improvised tables. He said, much too loudly, "Hey, that apple pie has a bug in it!"

His embarrassed mother tried to hush him, "Claud that's not a bug; it's just a seed."

"Humph, first seed I ever saw that had legs."

THE FIRST CHRISTMAS TREE LIGHTS

No one at college could imagine why I was so excited about selecting and buying several strings of lights for our Christmas tree at home. It was 1959, and it was the first year we had electricity at the ranch. The first time we were going to have lights on our tree was, indeed, a big deal to me!

The tree was a big and slightly crooked Ponderosa Pine that had been cut on the mountain behind the ranch house and hauled in by horseback.

When it came time to decorate this tree, all of my family joined in the occasion. We first put the star on top while the tree was lying on its side. Then we set the tree upright. Putting on all the other decorations was not easy because of the tree's large volume. Then it was time for the long-awaited lights to be put on! Never mind that I had not bought enough strands. Daddy thought we would enjoy the lighting of the tree most if we waited until it was dark. To us, this event was in the same category as flipping the switch on the national tree in Washington, D.C. The very first lighting of the tree at the ranch was indeed a beautiful and a thrilling event for all who gathered for the occasion.

THE CARBIDE MIXMASTER

It was not unusual for me to spend the weekend with one of my friends in "town." (I always wanted to be with them so we could do "town" things, namely go to the Saturday movie matinee!) Whenever I visited my town friends, I was quick to note the differences in lifestyles and the wonderful amenities that electricity provided. At the ranch, our lights were provided by carbide (which was ignited and burned like gas), and our refrigerator and cooking stove operated by butane. Since my mother spent much of her time in the kitchen, I wanted her to have modern conveniences just like my friends' moms had. I reported to mother after one of my city visits that I intended to invent for her a carbide Mixmaster!

A FAILURE TO IDENTIFY

The four of us—my husband, four-year-old daughter, two-and-a-half-year-old son, and I—were shopping at the main Naval Exchange store in Norfolk, Virginia. As was not unusual, one of the kids "escaped." Where was Anna? We began looking, frantically, and retracing our steps through various departments. In a few minutes a message went out over the intercom: "We have a little lost girl here and she needs to be claimed by her parents." We dashed over to the customer-service office and were relieved to see Anna sitting there. But…whoa! We did not look like her parents because Anna was Chinese and we obviously were not. The person in charge asked Anna if we were her parents…and she mischievously replied: "No!" We laughed, but then realized that this could be serious! After we produced identification and pictures, and our son added his two cents, the authorities released Anna to us. We held on tightly to her hand and made a hasty exit from the Exchange!

Life in the Big City

It being the correct thing to do, I wasted no time in finding a suitable Baptist Church where I could move my church membership. Being a student at Texas Christian University in Fort Worth was a far cry from being a member of the 128-member congregation in Balmorhea, my hometown. Nonetheless, I liked the large Travis Avenue Baptist Church, and the members there were very friendly. On a given Sunday, during the time of "invitation," I went down the aisle and expressed to the pastor my desire to move my church membership from Balmorhea to Travis Avenue. He shook my hand and gave me an information card to complete. At the close of the invitation, the pastor took the card to present me to the congregation. He began to read, struggling with the pronunciation of Balmorhea, "BAL-MORE-RAY...is that close?"

"No sir," I replied. "It's about 480 miles from here."

A soft chuckle rippled throughout the assembly. But they did let me join!

Bringing in the Sheaves

I had a notion when I was a child that I was a true intellectual. This was an idea I was eager to promote and maintain (without effort, of course).

In the general knowledge of farmyards, I knew there was another term for pigs or hogs, and that it started with the letter "S." What I couldn't figure out was WHY in our church services we so frequently sang about those stupid pigs! The hymn sounded forth, "…we shall come rejoicing, bringing in the sheaves."

It took me a long time to confess my error when I found out the "S" word was "swine" and sheaves were bundles of wheat from the harvest!

LSMFT

Back in the late 1940s and early 1950s there were not many tobacco companies manufacturing cigarettes. Those that were around were in strong competition for the market. Lucky Strike began using LSMFT (Lucky Strike Means Fine Tobacco) in advertising jingles and printed advertisements. My politically opinionated dad developed his own translation of the catchy phrase… he said it meant, "Lord, Save Me From Truman."

Uncle Ed Comes Home

World War II was over! Uncle Edmond was coming home! He had been held in Japan as a prisoner of war for forty-one months, and for quite some time, none of the family even knew if he was alive. I was three years old at the time. The great day of his homecoming arrived, and all the family (even those like me that he didn't know about) gathered at the farmhouse in Robert Lee. Everyone chattered, cried, and waited anxiously for Uncle Edmond's car to come driving up the dusty lane. My take on it all: "My, he would be glad to see all these WICKED faces."

No one could figure out what I really meant, but it did break the tension, and the retelling of my observation did amuse Uncle Ed when he came home to us all!

The Days of Radio

Our battery-operated radio was one of our best friends during my growing up years. Every weekday morning around six, my daddy tuned to a farm-and-ranch report given by Henry Howell on station WOAI in San Antonio. One day my brother, about four at the time, announced that he could spell "San Antonio" (spelling being a BIG DEAL in our household). My mother encouraged him, but reminded him that it was a long name to spell correctly. He assured all of us he could do it.

"Go ahead then, son," my mother replied.
"Okay…W-O-A-I San-Antonio."

All Those Beans!

Aunt Nora lived in Manhattan, just about in the middle of the Big Apple, but she did come home to her native Texas for visits from time to time. On one such trip, she was to bring her totally Yankee roommate Kay with her. We all geared up for "Kay's visit to Texas," as we wanted her to go back to New York with a favorable impression.

After staying with us for some time, Kay reported to her anxiously awaiting friends up North that Texas homemakers did a very strange thing: "When they got out the dried pinto beans (normally called frijoles) to prepare for cooking, they poured a large amount out on the table and counted them before raking them off into a bowl or pot."

Aunt Nora assured her that the beans were NOT being counted, but picked over for rocks, dirt clods, and sticker burrs! The preparation of dried beans for cooking is still referred to as "counting the beans" among family members.

KAISER BILL

A rather prominent landmark on the north side of the ranch is a mountain with a tall rock formation at its peak. The configuration of it looks very much like a WW I German army helmet. Hence, Daddy dubbed it "Kaiser Peak". Daddy's little ditty about it:

Kaiser Bill went up the hill to take a peek at France;
Kaiser Bill came down the hill with bullets in his pants!

Westward Ho the Camels Go

During his latter years, my grandpa Kingston fascinated us younger family members with his stories of "the camels." Before the Civil War, Jefferson Davis was Secretary of War in the Buchanan Administration. Jefferson Davis thought it would be a workable plan to improve trade to the west by employing camels as pack animals. The camels were imported, and Davis sent them to Camp Verde. The plan was to use the animals for Army supply and overland transportation. Caravans were assembled, and the treks through the desert southwest were to begin. But wait a minute! Those camels were NOT English speaking, nor were they anything like milk cows or mules. Army troops had great difficulty managing them, so some Arab handlers were quickly brought in to get the beasts moving in the right direction—in fact, to get them moving at all!

The route of the camel trains was well known; so many people came to see the strange animals and the camel handlers who wore "tablecloths." Middle Eastern names were difficult for most folks, as was the name of the main man among the camel drivers. He came to be called simply "Hai Jolly." As a small boy, my grandpa Kingston got to see Hai Jolly and the camels.

The camels fared no better than the Confederacy, the government's plan to employ them being eventually abandoned. Most of the camels were turned adrift into the wilderness. Many of them subsequently died in the areas of the trip west that were rocky and mountainous, and others were killed off.

THUMBING YOUR WAY THROUGH BALMORHEA

Even back in the 1950s, not everyone would pick up hitchhikers, but sometimes my daddy would. One such day, he was returning from Pecos. Along about Verhalen, he spotted a fellow hitchhiking with a big bag. Daddy pulled over. He explained to the fellow that he wasn't going too much farther, but he could give him a lift to the upper valley. The fellow tossed his bag into the back of the pickup and got in the cab. The stranger said that he had not been able to find *any* work and was on his way to California because he was certain work would be available there. Daddy then offered him a few days' work at the ranch; the man quickly declined the offer. At this point, daddy asked, "What is it that you do?"

Forthrightly the hitchhiker replied, "I am a ballet dancer."

Daddy abruptly slammed on the brakes, pulled off the road, and told the guy, "Well, you get out of here and dance right on down the road, then."

THE GIRLS VS. MR. MCCOY

Balmorhea is a small high school, so certain groups can command a good bit of attention. Such was the case of the girls' basketball team in the late 1950s. First of all, there was a new coach! He was single, fairly good looking, and Balmorhea was his first job out of college. It did not take long for things to go sour! Coach McCoy had rules—I mean LOTS of rules—affecting things we were certain did not require any rules! But we did want to keep playing basketball, and we did want to win. There was an inordinate amount of "gritching" from both sides.

Finally it happened: Mr. McCoy had come up with a rule deemed supremely goofy and unnecessary by the girls. He wanted us to pull our blue and white sweat socks up to our knees, and then hold them in place with blue kneepads, whether we were wearing the white uniforms or the blue ones. The team objected because those knee-high socks got hot and scratchy. Also, if you were moving around like you ought to be, the socks kept slipping down, more or less acting as hobbles. In addition, it just didn't look good. We girls decided that if Mr. McCoy wanted leg coverings, we would give him leg coverings! The plan was to shave our legs except for an inch-wide strip on the outside of our legs, from the knee to the ankle. We didn't say a thing, and after about eight to ten days of hair growing, it was time to put the plan into action.

A big game with an archrival would be in our gymnasium, which meant we would be wearing white. A big crowd was expected. Team introductions were made, visitors first. Then we all lined up on the court, our "leg sideburns" very prominent. Boing! It all hit Coach McCoy. His eyes got big, his face got red, and he started swinging a towel around. He couldn't bench us all because he did not want to forfeit the game. It did not take long for the student body and hometown crowd to start clapping and yelling. The game HAD to go on. We did win, and yes, we did shave the leg sideburns—but Mr. McCoy discarded some of his rules, too!

THE DOWNFALL OF THE THREE MUSKETEERS

It was Spring and time for the area-wide ladies prayer retreat at Highland Lakes Baptist Encampment. It is a beautiful facility in a rural area of the Hill Country near Marble Falls.

There were about twenty ladies in the cabin to which I was assigned. The second evening we all prepared to go to the 7:30 PM service. The last one out failed to shut the door securely, so an unwanted visitor awaited us upon our return to the cabin. I was the first to enter and soon realized there was a skunk in the middle of the sleeping area. Having grown up on a ranch, I was somewhat familiar with certain wild varmints, and I knew there had better be some quick and correct action or serious trouble was at hand. First, I turned to the other ladies and in a hushed voice said, "No screaming! Just back up, ladies, and don't panic. Please stay out of the way!"

Very quietly I moved into the cabin where I discovered Mr. SKUNK pilfering through some candy and gum he had found in an open suitcase. He looked up but didn't seem startled. I inched close enough to get some of the candy and made a trail of it right out the door. I was able to get behind him and hurry him along, ever so gently. He finally ambled out into the cool night air. The ladies cheered, except for the lady whose candy the skunk had taken, who said, "He took the Three Musketeers bar and that is my favorite one!"

That was enough adventure for one night!

DY-NO-MITE!

Daddy had been looking over the ranch for the ideal place to construct a major stock tank, one that would be deep and have a B-I-G dirt dam. He decided that the perfect location for the tank would be about two and a half miles north of the ranch house at the head of Wildcat Draw so that Chalk Draw, Maverick Draw, and Good Enough Draw could feed into the tank when the rare rains came to that part of Texas. Next, he had to secure a "cat man," meaning a Caterpillar operator, who knew how to move rocks and dirt and make a fine stock tank. Dick Langer signed on for the job. He was not a local fellow and had no family, so he lived at the ranch house with us while he worked on the tank.

The Caterpillar and dump trucks were not enough; some dynamite was needed. The crates of dynamite acquired were in thick wooden boxes with dovetailed sides holding them together. Needless to say, those twenty-inch cubes were heavy! Work on the tank progressed, and so did a nice surprise for me! Dick Langer thought those heavy-duty dynamite boxes were too good to waste. He designed and made me a play cabinet, complete with doors, drawers, and open-hutch shelves.

Being six, I was delighted; so much so, in fact, that I took it upon myself to help him finish it. One day while he was over at the tank, I went to our basement and found some blue paint and some white paint, and a paintbrush. Never mind that the cabinet had not been sanded and was not ready to be painted. Shelves and inside quickly became blue and exterior parts became white, with a few smudges and drips overlapping on the color scheme. Whew! Mother and Daddy were really annoyed with me, but Mr. Langer was not. He said patiently, "It's her cabinet anyway, and if she wanted to paint it like that, it's okay by me."

After about four months, the tank was completed; we named it "Dam Dick" and waited for rain! Dick Langer left us, and we never saw him again; the big stock tank and the dynamite box cabinet are still with us. That cabinet has gone to its fourth owner, my great neice, Kinney. It still has the same "finish," and you can still read the words stamped on those dynamite boxes through my original, unprofessional paint job.

Bad Hair Day

My mother always had one comment to make to people whose hair was messed up or had an uncombed look: "You look like you combed your hair with an egg beater."

Why It Wouldn't Rain

Rain has always been a very desirable commodity in the Davis Mountains of West Texas. It was not uncommon for ranchers to check out the clouds and call one another on the phone to see what it looked like on the other side of the mountain regarding the possibilities of getting some rain. Allene, the long time employee of Ernest and Faye Hunsucker, had become part of the local pattern of "weather watchers."

For several consecutive days, the clouds had been in abundance and looked so promising to yield the much-needed rain, but not a drop had fallen. Along about the fifth day, the thunderclouds formed up Madera Canyon, but no rain. Allene went to check one more time before the sun set. She came back into the house with her explanation about the failure of those clouds to produce: "Ah declare, Miz Faye, them clouds is just constipated."

The Dating Game

Growing up out on the ranch meant I spent an extensive amount of time with adults. I quite frequently included myself in their activities and conversations. When I was five, one of my mother's sisters, Aunt Margie, was living with us. She had been going out with Cecil Lewis, a likable cowboy from a neighboring ranch. On one of those "meddling" occasions, I was present when Aunt Margie was discussing her upcoming date for that night. When she began getting ready to go out, I also began to get dressed, comb my hair, etc. She asked what I thought I was doing; I informed her (shocked that she would even ask!) that I was getting ready to go out with her and Cecil Lewis. "Oh no! You're not going," she said.

I stomped my foot, looked her in the eye, and retorted, "The hell I'm not!"

I didn't get to go—not that time, anyway!

THE *REAL* ERNIE PYLE

No one really knew where the doorstop for the white bedroom had originated, or why it ended up at the ranch. It never seemed appropriate nor to fit in with any of the ranch house decor. This doorstop was a foot-high figure of a swashbuckling pirate. He wore a big black hat with crossbones on it, loop earrings, and a pistol stuffed in the waist of his trousers. He held a drawn sword and had a wooden leg. In other words, he was a buccaneer, not a buckaroo! He had just always been there.

I asked mother the pirate's name, and she said he really did not have one. Now this seemed totally unacceptable to me. I gave it lengthy consideration before I came up with a name I was certain mother would permit me to give my pirate friend. Since she read and admired the works of the late war correspondent Ernie Pyle, I just knew she would be delighted that I chose to name the pirate "Ernie Pyle."

That doorstop is now in my home, and some fifty-five years later, all is well with Ernie Pyle.

SALLY RAND AND PATTY LAMA

It was not unusual for us to take in "doggies" (orphaned animals) and raise them to adulthood. There were two particular ones that were given their names because of the characteristics they each exhibited. Sally, the Pronghorn antelope, was named after Sally Rand, a well-known "Fan Dancer" of an earlier time. The antelope's "fan" was the two-inch long, white hair on her behind that would bristle outward (fan out) when she became frightened. I did not know who or what Sally Rand was, but Daddy *did,* and he deemed it a good name for the little antelope.

The lamb, on the other hand, was something else! To put it bluntly, she was a glutton, and one with bad manners at that! The fellow for whom the lamb was named also fit that description. Patty Lama and his wife were itinerant folks trying to get to Oregon, so they were working at the ranch for a few weeks. Mother included the two of them at mealtime, but only about twice! Mr. Lama's table manners were so atrocious that mother did not want us to see such a sight or possibly to be influenced by him! That lamb also could not get enough to eat! She would smack and gulp and frequently pull the nipple off her bottle of milk. Then she would run over to Sally and try to steal her bottle!

After a few weeks, the Lama couple moved on west. The lamb and the antelope grew up together, quite a strange pair. Sally was quick and agile; Patty was homely and awkward. As full-grown animals, they went their separate ways. Sally was shipped in a very special crate to the Fort Worth Zoo. We even visited her there, and she still knew us! Patty rejoined the other sheep on the ranch and raised a number of lambs. I'm betting they all survived, because they were just like Patty!

TWO BITS, FOUR BITS, SIX BITS, A DOLLAR

I was not a cheerleader at Balmorhea High, but I was president of the Pep Squad. One of my primary duties was to keep an ongoing list of cheers and let the cheerleaders know when to do certain ones and to keep the cheerleaders from getting into a rut. (If they kept doing the same old yells, it would have become boring, and the Pep Squad would have lost enthusiasm, therefore making it difficult to do our job to cheer the boys on to victory.)

Probably, no one would make a study of school cheers, other than to note that "times have changed." The truth is, some of the '50s cheers are now utterly obsolete:

"Bob Hope, Betty Grable
Come on boys,
we know you're able."

"He's the peaches, he's the cream,
He's the captain* of our team." (*coach, back, leader)

"Sittin' on a milk can
Beatin' on a tin can
Who can?
We can
Nobody else can!"

Cheerleaders:	"How do ya like your oysters?"
Pep Squad:	"Raw, raw, raw."
Cheerleaders:	"How do ya like your cabbage?"
Pep Squad:	"Slaw, slaw, slaw."
Cheerleaders:	"How do ya like your sugar?"
Pep Squad:	"Sweet, sweet, sweet."
Cheerleaders:	"How do ya like the Eagles?" (or other team)
Pep Squad:	"Beat, beat, beat."

It goes without saying, but it was mandatory for every good pep squad to have a few retaliatory yells in their repertoire, just in case the other team's cheerleaders and pep squad got ugly. If they did it first, we needed to be prepared to respond and defend school honor. We were, indeed, prepared:

"California oranges
Arizona cactus
We play the Lions (or other team)
Just for practice!"

"Chew tobacco, chew tobacco
Spit on the wall
The boys from Pyote (or other team)
Can't play ball."

"I'm a raindrop,
I'm a raindrop
From the sky,
But I'd rather be
A raindrop
Than a drip
From Toyah High (or other team)."

Since Balmorhea played six-man football, some of the cheers from the standard manual on high school cheers did not fit because the authors and publishers just assumed that everybody played eleven-man football. In the six-man game, fifteen-yards gain is required from the line of scrimmage to get a first down, so "First and ten, do it again," was out! So was,

"The team was in a huddle The captain lowered his head
They all got together and this is what they said:
End, center, tackle, guard
Hit your man and hit him hard.
Hit him high; hit him low, Come on Bears, let's go!"
Excuse me! With only six guys, there is no tackle or guard!

GREAT DAY AT THE STUDENT UNION

My first roommate at TCU, in the fall of 1959, was a tall, thin, blond, art major who chain-smoked. She was into intellectual pursuits and cared nothing about "jock chasing." However…there was one Big Man on Campus who she watched carefully. She didn't want to date him or anything like that, but she did covet the mint green, sleeveless shirt with white, knit trim at the armholes and v-neck that Don Floyd frequently wore. It seemed to be his uniform of choice with which to saunter through the student union to check out the female portion of the campus population. Phyllis talked about that shirt, and how she would like to wear it, and how good it would make her tan look.

 No reason not to put a plan into action. I didn't know Don Floyd, but I definitely knew he was a great football player and would not give me the time of day. Next best thing, I did know the trainer for the Horned Frogs football team, George Roach. I told him about Phyllis' thing for Don's mint-green shirt. The deal was this: if he got me the shirt, Phyllis had to wear it to the Student Union at an appointed time. George sneaked the shirt to me, laundered and ready to wear. Phyllis was ecstatic! She had no qualms about wearing it in public. As she was tall, the shirt's tail came well above her knees. The v-neck was not too plunging, but the arm holes were too large. So with minor adjustments, nothing to deface "the shirt," Phyllis made her visit to the Student Union. Don Floyd was waiting, as were most of the football team and the rest of us "busy bodies." Phyllis modeled the shirt, worn with one of her pencil thin skirts and a wide belt. She and Don had a Coke, talked awhile, and we all quit staring. I washed the shirt, gave it back to George Roach, and it wasn't long before it made an appearance again as Floyd's favorite leisure shirt, none the worse for Phyllis' having worn it!

THE SECRET WEAPON

The coach of the middle school (Junior High back in those days) football team was a young guy out of Midwestern University. His name was Don Phillips, but he liked to look and sound tough, so the students, among themselves, called him "Killer." Balmorhea was playing Barstow and winning rather handily. In fact, the game had become boring. Killer realized it was up to him to bring some kind of spark to this contest. He had been convinced that the referees were not doing the best job, and that they, too, were bored.

It's true in six-man football that positions and play calling are a bit different than eleven-man. Dennis Turnbough was the center for this particular Balmorhea team and he did just that: center the ball to the quarterback, then block the defensive team's line. Killer came up with a bold plan. During a time out, he told the boys he was putting in a new play that they had never tried before. The boys listened, broke the huddle with an onrush of enthusiasm, and set up to run Killer's new play. It was a "center keeper." Dennis did not hike the ball. While the other team was looking around in bewilderment, Dennis untracked those long legs of his and ran for the touchdown! Unfortunately, the referees got back into the game enough to realize that "center keeper" was an illegal procedure. So, not only did Dennis' only touchdown NOT count, but the Balmorhea team also was penalized ten yards from the line of scrimmage. Let's hear it for innovative play calling!

Not Here, Man!

As a present for graduating from Balmorhea High School in 1963, my brother and his long time friend, Charlie Oats, went to New York City to visit Aunt Nora. These two boys were both pure country, but Charlie was the epitome of a small-town Texas boy: six-foot-three, lanky, sandy hair, freckles, low-slung Levis, and unpolished boots.

The boys were staying in a hotel a couple of blocks from Aunt Nora's apartment. She lived on the eighth floor, so they made frequent elevator trips. On one such trip, going down, Charlie pulled out his pocketknife with a four-inch blade and began to clean his fingernails. Whoa! I don't think so! There was major panic among the other passengers on that elevator. One grabbed Charlie, one pushed the alarm button, and two women screamed. My brother got so tickled he was no help either to Charlie or to the situation. In his slow Texas drawl, Charlie apologized and reassured the folks that he didn't mean any harm, and he had no intention of doing anything wrong. He was merely practicing good grooming habits. He quickly folded up the pocketknife and slid it back into his pocket. There it remained until he returned to Texas, where folks understand good hygiene!

THE NEW PUPPY

One of my cousins and his wife made the decision to add a dog to their family. It was not long until a "free-to-good-home," mostly German shepherd puppy became available. Jerry, Cindy, and their young daughter excitedly welcomed the eight-week-old dog. First order of business: give the wiggly creature a name. "Polly" was the moniker chosen. Aside from feeding, watering, brushing, and playing with the rawhide bone, the major task at hand was the "house breaking" training. Oh my! This aspect of dog ownership did *not* go well! My cousin read books, talked to the vet, conferred among his friends, and still could not find the secret to teaching that dog where was the acceptable place to go to the bathroom, namely outside. It became so bad that they changed the dog's name to "Polly-urine-thing!"

How to Remember a Name

It was one of those classic anxious moments. I was trying to prepare my daddy to meet a very special boyfriend of mine, Dick Bettle. Dick was coming down to the ranch for a visit. I had extolled Dick's virtues, but to help Daddy remember Dick's last name, I explained that it was B-E-T-T-L-E, like "K e t t l e."

Dick came to the ranch, the visit went well, and after he left, I was asking Daddy how he liked my friend. He said, "You know, that Bill Platter is a fine fellow." So much for my helpful hints!

YOU CAN'T OUTHURT A HYPOCHONDRIAC

In the course of his lifetime, Daddy did sustain some severe injuries and endure some major pain. But also, he was not going to be outdone. No matter what your ailment at the moment, his problem was going to be worse, and therefore, command more attention. My mother would never let him forget an example of this that occurred on March 11, 1946. Daddy had gotten up early that morning, taken his hunting hounds, and joined some neighboring ranchers to go hunt down a wolf that had been killing baby lambs. It had been a long, difficult day of riding horseback, and the men still had not found the wolf. Daddy came home tired and hungry. Mother fed him supper, then gave him the news that it was time for her to go to the hospital in Pecos (fifty-five miles from the ranch) to give birth to the baby she was expecting.

He did not get in a dither; he did not panic. His comment as he prepared to make the trip to Pecos: "Well, Momma, I hope you aren't in as much pain as I am right now. That wolf hunt really hurt me."

He got no sympathy this time! After several hours of intense labor, mother gave birth to my brother on March 12.

Nosy Nellie Gets in Trouble

Mother was awakened during the night by a small commotion beside the bed. A mouse had fallen into the wastepaper basket and couldn't get out. Since it was the middle of the night, mother decided to put a magazine over the wastepaper basket and take care of the rodent in the morning. I hadn't yet dressed for the day when mother prepared to take the mouse out to the back yard to dump it out so the eager cat could take care of it. As I kept trying to peer into the basket to see, mother told me that I had better get back and stay out of the way. I did not move away, but only got closer! Mother removed the magazine and tipped the basket so the mouse would come tumbling out, and I bent even nearer. I did not want to miss anything. That mouse was not about to become easy prey for the cat! Instead, he ran straight up my pajamas' leg! I took off, running stiff-legged across the back yard and yelling. Mother got so tickled! Who knows where that mouse ended up? But for certain, he was not the cat's breakfast that particular morning.

Not Exactly Heloise

Now Daddy may have been a cowboy and a rancher, but he had some sure-fire household hints, about which he felt strongly. Never mind that he did NOT do housework, sort the laundry, nor cook. He was quick to share information he considered incontrovertible fact with friends, relatives, and total strangers. If you needed to know, he was going to tell you! All this was for your own good, naturally.

The rule for biscuits: 1) open biscuit into halves; 2) place on plate, fluffy sides up; 3) apply your choice of accouterments (gravy, jelly, syrup, honey, etc.); 4) turn biscuits over, with crust sides up; 5) cut in suitable bite-size pieces and enjoy. Step four is the critical step. By following this procedure, one avoided having the biscuit slide off the plate, make a mess, or have the fork clank loudly against the plate.

Following in this same line was the use of syrup and honey. Whatever your choice, you were NOT to drip said liquid, nor let it run down the side of the container. The penalty for this offense was a stern lecture and maybe even a little finger shaking.

It was the duty of everyone who liked sweetened iced tea to use saccharin. (Remember, this was before any other sugar substitutes were made.) In fact, Daddy was so intent on everyone using those little pills that he would get a teaspoon and crush the tablets in the spoon with the handle of his knife, then deposit them in the goblets used to serve tea at our house. What was the reason for the non-use of sugar? Because those who used sugar did not stir it up adequately, and it left a mess in the bottom of the glass, and that in turn made it hard for the person washing the dishes to get the glass clean! Did Daddy ever wash the dishes? No, he did not!

One can pour a liquid a right way or a wrong way. It was Daddy's guess that you would do it the wrong way, unless he told you otherwise. The correct way to pour: arrange both containers in correct proximity. When you begin pouring, do it quickly; no dribbling or dripping. When the transfer of liquid is complete, STOP quickly. Set the pouring container down on the table or counter, making sure it is far enough from the edge so as not to be knocked over.

THE COWBOYS VS. THE COOK

A couple of cowboys, new to the ranch, came in to have their supper. Grandma Kingston had done up a hearty meal for them. She set out a fresh pound of butter that she had churned and molded that morning. When the biscuits were brought from the wood-burning stove, those men started buttering a pile of the biscuits while they were hot. Their mistake was cutting the butter off each end of the one-pound rectangle. Grandma promptly reminded those cow herders that they should cut the butter off just one end and not mess it up and make it look like she hadn't molded it properly during the butter-making process.

Never missing a bite of his well-buttered biscuit, one of the men replied, "Shoot, Miz Kingston, what difference does it make? We're gonna eat it all anyway!"

The Facts

Our daughter, Anna, was in the third grade at Quantico Elementary School. Her best friend's name was Anna Grace, and she lived in a housing area across the highway from our military quarters.

One day Anna Grace came to school with MUCH to report. She had seen her mother and daddy making love and had been so intrigued that she stayed around and caught the whole show! Now she wanted to compare her newly acquired data with whatever Anna might know and be willing to share.

At that point, our Anna had little scandalous information; she just knew right terminology as compared to gutter terms, and some basic technical things. So, in the quiet of the evening with just the two of us, Anna asked me a number of questions. Mainly, she wanted to know if Anna Grace was telling the truth or had just made it up. We went through it all, and I added to her knowledge in what I deemed a thorough, but not a frightening or a too explicit, manner.

Anna got very quiet, took a deep breath, looked me squarely in the eye, and said, with voice quivering, "Does your mother know you do that?"

It Wasn't the Trend Back Then

Daddy kept several good hunting hounds at the ranch. It was not unusual for men from neighboring ranches to get together and go on a big hunt. This was especially true if there was evidence that a particular varmint had been killing or crippling domestic livestock.

It had been a long, tiring day for both the men and the dogs, so the men shot some jackrabbits on the way in to feed the dogs. By the time they got back to civilization, it was getting dark. One of the fellows tossed the rabbits into the back of Daddy's pickup, and those hounds jumped on their supper. Daddy did not think his dog Bud should be eating one rabbit and holding another one down with his foot. Therefore, Daddy reached down and grabbed the rabbit under Bud's foot to toss it to one of the other dogs. Bad idea! Bud thought another dog was trying to steal his rabbit. Once he had bitten, he realized it was Daddy, and he immediately dropped all rabbits and shook in fear.

When they got back into some light and applied rudimentary first aid, the men could see that the top of Daddy's left ear was bitten nearly off and was barely attached. The decision was made to get him on into town and see if they could rouse old Dr. Kelly to sew up Daddy's ear. Meanwhile the men were trying to stop the bleeding, clean things up, and transport Daddy.

Dr. Kelly was not enthusiastic about treating this wound. He was old and tired, and this injury was not life threatening. However, he got it together, adjusted his glasses, and did the stitching, then the bandaging. The bandage had to be changed several times over the next few days, and in about a week, Dr. Kelly removed the stitches.

Only one thing Dr. Kelly forgot to mention—he had not put in enough stitches. The ear had grown back together, but with a hole about the size of a number two pencil near the head!

Not many people bothered with lawsuits or criminal negligence back then. In fact, Daddy never got around to having the ear repaired or corrected. Instead, he had fun with it. He loved to gross out unsuspecting strangers or his nieces and nephews by allowing the ear piece of his gold wire reading glasses to hang through that hole instead of fitting properly over the back of his ear. He also liked to torment (in a mischievous way) my mother by telling her she could put a big ring through that hole and lead him around like a bull with a ring in his nose!

IS YOU IS OR IS YOU AIN'T?

Uncle Doug, my mother's brother, was the youngest boy and next-to-the-youngest child in a family of nine children. All nine of them agreed that their parents were more lenient and liberal with the younger ones. However, their father—Claud Dean—was very firm about certain rules of family conduct. One such rule required everyone's attendance at Sunday school and church.

One Sunday morning, the time to depart was fast approaching. Thirteen-year-old Doug was observed to be in a state of unpreparedness. When questioned by his mother about it, he informed her unequivocally that he was not going to Sunday school and church. His mother made no response to the impudent statement. She calmly went about getting everyone else ready to go. As she was ushering them all out the door, a dressed and ready-to-go Doug appeared. Acting surprised, his mother said, "Doug, I thought you were not going today."

"Well, I said I wasn't, but Daddy said I was, and in that case, I guess I am."

Just Some Ditties

In Spanish or in English, of his own creation or quoted from a source, Daddy liked ditties. Frequently, those he shared among his cronies were not suitable for repeating and certainly not suitable for printing in a book not considered "X" rated.

Daddy did not require any special occasion to share one of his rhymes or songs. He thought it very humorous to teach children these sayings; they in turn would repeat them, and then get in trouble! An example of just such a ditty:

Once upon a time on a streetcar line
a monkey chewed tobacco
and a goose drank wine.
The streetcar broke,
the monkey choked
and they all went to heaven
on a dead billy goat!

An original one he liked had to do with bad smelling things:

A pig and a skunk both got drunk,
then neither of them knew that the other one stunk.

Bodily functions have always been a source of humor in some company. This one is in the "keep it clean" camp:

Some folks I know can sneeze with a soft and gentle wheeze, but listen, brother, they run for cover the second time I sneeze.

FLING-WING VS. FIXED-WING

It was part of the job description for flight instructors at Naval Aviation Training in Pensacola, Florida, to preview the naval flight program for various university ROTC cadets and midshipmen. This was best accomplished by providing the cadets and midshipmen short introductory-type flights in the basic flight training aircraft. My husband, Captain Bettle, USMC helicopter and fixed-wing pilot, was one of those instructors. It was his turn to take some of the cadets out to fly. They were an enthusiastic group and had numerous questions. One of the young men very nearly got bounced off the flight before he even got on the plane when he said to my Vietnam-veteran husband, "Do you fly helicopters, or are you a real pilot?"

THE TRIP NEXT DOOR

While my husband was stationed in Pensacola as a flight student, we lived in a two-bedroom rental house. Our landlord and his family lived next door. The very winsome four-year-old boy of the family frequently knocked at our back door. He liked to visit me because I was nearly always home, gave him undivided attention, and frequently made cookies! Frankie was no real bother to me, but we did have one problem: his mother did not always know where he was! She would eventually retrieve him and confront him with, "Why didn't you ask me if you could go next door?"

Frankie always had the same defense: "I got forgot."

Five Feet High and Rising

Just as there was a certain time of the year for cattle roundup in West Texas, there was also a time for the ranch folks to go to Camp Meeting. You might call it a spiritual roundup!

It was in June, around 1912, and the Baptists had all packed their wagons and tents and headed for Madera Canyon. What a fine meeting this promised to be! George W. Truett, the Billy Graham of his day, was to be the main speaker. Things were under way, and then it set in to raining. We are not talking about a late afternoon thundershower. It was a real frog strangler! The rains came down, and the floods came up. With Madera Canyon filling fast with raging water and bouncing boulders, the Camp Meeting attendees had to make a swift retreat back down the canyon.

Will and Annie Kingston, whose ranch headquarters was about three miles away, realized the plight of the folks up the canyon, so Will rode out to meet them and invited them to come on over to the ranch house.

Not everyone decided to stay, but a large number did. The two-story, nine-bedroom house was put to the test. The center hall was 35 x 15 feet. By pushing aside tables and non-essential furniture and dragging in the dining room chairs, a "sanctuary" was set up. The horses and pack mules were taken care of at the large corral. The people spread out their food in the huge formal dining room. When everyone was dry and in a non-panic frame of mind, the Rev. George W. Truett held forth in the ranch-house hallway!

THE BIG ONE

A major part of the 4-H Club program in rural Texas had to do with club members raising, grooming, and training farm animals for competition at livestock shows. These usually began with local or county shows. The prize-winning animals then advanced to larger, regional shows. Competition was stiff, but the sale premiums were good if you were fortunate enough to place high enough to make the sale at the major shows. To country kids, Big D (Dallas) in October at State Fair time was the ultimate place to be and to show an animal.

In 1956 Reeves County had enough qualifying livestock, steers, and lambs, to warrant a trip to the State Fair. What a place! Hundreds of cattle, sheep, and pigs; the Midway with its giant roller coaster; the exhibition halls; and entertainment from Joey Chitwood's daredevil driving to the Ice Capades were all there to engulf us!

Mother was doing some shopping and helping other parents with meals for us over at the big van. Daddy, however, was taking in the Fair and helping us keep things running smoothly with the livestock. We were responsible for keeping things clean and attractive around our animals. We were waiting for the hay wagon to bring our fresh straw so we could re-do it for the areas where our calves were tethered. The driver finally came, and he was apologetic about the straw. He said, "I know you all ordered buck wheat, but we don't have that fancy stuff, we just have this oat straw. Will that do?"

"No, no, we didn't ask for buck wheat, that's just the name of our County Agent. Mr. Buck Wheat ordered straw or hay, but he did not care what kind it was," we explained to him.

Hay delivered, we then set to work laying down the clean, fresh straw.

My daddy had waited to go to the restroom until the hay issue was settled, so the minute it was, he took off down the long aisle to the center section where the restrooms were located. The first sign he saw was WOMEN, then he turned the corner, and Daddy figured the next door with a sign on it would be MEN, so he dashed right on into that second facility. NOT men's—it was COLORED WOMEN. Daddy expressed his apologies and beat a hasty retreat. He very carefully read the third sign BEFORE entering!

THE SWIMMING POOL

My grandfather figured that if you were going to build a water tank for storage, irrigating a garden, and for livestock, it might as well serve yet another purpose—a swimming pool. So, just the other side of the big corral, a couple of hundred yards from the ranch house, he built *the swimming pool*. It was made of rock and cement, had a shallow end of about 3 ½ feet and a deep end of 7 feet. The bottom was semi-smooth cement, and there were steps in the east corner of the shallow end. This pool/tank was 30 feet wide and 100 feet long, fed by cold spring water; there was no filter, no chlorine, no Jacuzzi.

There was a fence just beyond the swimming pool with a gate that led into the big pasture. One day Mother and Daddy had driven the nine miles around the mountain to a neighbor's. Daddy's legs were mostly incapacitated, so mother was doing both the driving and the gate opening and shutting, which was a bit of a chore for one person to handle. On the way back home, Daddy told Mother that if she could open the gate, he believed he could get his leg over and press the gas pedal to drive through the gate for her, then she could shut the gate and drive on up to the house. Mother got out and opened the gate, and Daddy did drive through it.

But he didn't stop there! His foot got stuck—he couldn't move it, couldn't put on the brake, and couldn't turn the steering wheel. With dust and gravel flying, and my mother yelling and trying to catch the red pickup, Daddy plowed through the wire fence and was headed straight for the swimming pool. Mother was sure the pickup would come to a banging stop when it hit the rock and cement side of the swimming pool. Whoa Nellie! It did not! That old Ford truck launched into the air and landed, right-side-up, in the shallow end.

When Mother determined Daddy was not injured and could stay afloat, she ran to the house and got Pete, the hired man who was practically family, to come help. He was totally shocked when he got there and saw Daddy and the truck in the pool, but he swam out and helped Daddy out of the pickup and out of the pool. Mother had driven back down to the pool in the car, so the three of them made it back to the house, dried off, and called the wrecker service to come from town to get the red pickup out of the swimming pool. The man who came was most eager to hear the whole story about how Duncan and the truck ended up in the pool. It was a pretty far-fetched tale. After some drying out, the pickup ran just fine. Pete had to repair the fence, but everything else was okay. In fact, Daddy contended that it was the cleanest that red truck had been since it was new!

We All Loved Elvis

What an awesome adventure! It was Christmas time, and we were driving out to Grand Canyon, Arizona, to spend the holidays with Aunt Della, Bill, and the two boys. The trip was long, but the Canyon was beautiful, and there was a good bit of snow at the rim.

We soon got caught up in the holiday spirit and preparations for the big day—only we didn't know we were going to be in on a conspiracy. Aunt Della engaged our help to pull a trick on Bill. He had a total disdain for the fast rising star of rock 'n roll, Elvis Presley. Aunt Della's plan was to give Bill an Elvis record, wrapped up in a gorgeous package, of course. After his anticipated hostile reaction to that, then she would give him his real present, which was a new medical bag. We laughed, agreed to purchase an Elvis record of our choice, and would make certain it was wrapped and placed under the tree.

Next, Bill called us aside when Aunt Della was upstairs and asked for our assistance in pulling a joke on Aunt Della. He indicated that she had a major dislike and disgust for Elvis and his music. He thought it would be hilarious to get her the newest Elvis 45 record, wrap it up in a beautiful package, and put it under the tree for her Christmas!

We could hardly contain ourselves, we were so tickled about this double-barreled intrigue. We managed to carry out both sides of the plot and await present-opening time. Bill opened his Elvis record first. He looked at Aunt Della, who was trying to be sincere and loving then he looked at us, thinking we had made a mistake and put the wrong nametag on the gift. That, in fact, it was supposed to be FROM him, not TO him. With a calm but sour-looking expression on his face, he stuck the record back out of the way and moved on to other packages. Well, Aunt Della tore through the ornate wrappings only to discover that she, too, had an Elvis Presley record! It took a few seconds for her to realize what had happened. She and Bill both figured out that we knew and were in on the whole gag. By that time everyone was laughing. Bill liked his much-needed medical bag, and Aunt Della ended up with a lovely aquamarine ring. As for Elvis, he didn't fare so well; both those records were broken with a hammer and dumped into the trashcan!

NEVER A DULL MOMENT

It was a small, close-knit community. Of course, any group of strangers would be noticed and would arouse a certain amount of interest as to who they were, why they were there, and how long they would stay.

This particular group appeared out of the blue on a quiet winter day just after Christmas. The four men and two women checked into the two westernmost cabins of Uncle Charlie Splitgarber's motel about six miles west of Balmorhea on the El Paso highway.

They were not the church social type, but the group mingled enough to get invited out to the Kingston Ranch. The big, old ranch house was warm in the chill of the winter days, and the hospitality was friendly without being invasive. But, best of all, the ranch was a wonderful place to shoot all kinds of guns, including machine guns, without causing too much suspicion. Also, when one of the girls jumped in the car and honked the horn, everyone else would come running and jump in or stand on the running board. Then the six of them would roar off in the big, chrome-plated Buick in a cloud of gravel and dust. They would return in a few minutes, laughing and clapping. The local gentry did not really get to know this bunch very well, but the folks liked them. Heck! They were fun, and they dropped big bucks at local businesses!

Poof! In just a few weeks, the six vanished as quickly as they had arrived. There was no trace of them, or of their intended destination. The mystery was solved when newspapers reported that John Dillinger and his gang were arrested in Tucson, Arizona, and all sent back to the Midwest.

This was pretty much the last soiree for the Dillinger gang. Dillinger himself was sent to Indiana's Crown Point jail to await trial for bank holdups and the murder of Patrolman O'Malley. Three others went to Lima, Ohio, to answer for a multitude of bank robberies and the death of Sheriff Sarber. Baby Face Nelson was shot by two FBI agents. Homer Van Meter was gunned down in St. Paul. And the women? Billie Frechette was sentenced to two years in prison. Anna Sage was deported to Romania.

UNCLE CHARLIE'S MODEL T

Uncle Charlie and Aunt Tillie Splitgarber had a new Model T Ford. They proudly drove it everywhere. This particular model was the first one to have an electric starter button on it. It also maintained the customary hand crank on the outside front of the vehicle as a means of starting the motor. Being a rather old-fashioned man, Uncle Charlie insisted on using the hand crank to fire up and get going.

On one occasion, the two of them cranked up the Model T and ventured forth. It had rained earlier in the day, so there was water in a low-water crossing they had to forge. Uncle Charlie decided to risk it and go on through the water. They made it across, but the engine sputtered and stopped running. Uncle Charlie got out and began turning the crank, but all to no avail; the car wouldn't start. Uncle Charlie was quickly tiring. Aunt Tillie finally called out to him, "Charlie, why don't you try the commencer button?"

He did, the car started, and they were soon on their way.

The Lead Necklaces

In the rural settings of the West, folk medicine and the practice of it were fairly common. My father had one particular "cure" that he swore was certain to work: the wearing of lead necklaces to prevent nosebleeds. My brother and I both had frequent nosebleeds when we were young, around ages six to nine.

Daddy measured off a suitable length of cotton twine to go around each of our necks and tie. Then he cut the lead end off some bullets. Each of us got six or seven pieces. With a hammer, he shaped them onto the twine and tied it around our necks. We did not remove our necklaces to sleep, bathe, go swimming, or anything else that wasn't a dire emergency. Did they work? I wouldn't swear to it, but my daddy certainly believed these lead necklaces prevented a lot of nose bleeds that my brother and I would have had!

The Betty Crocker Award

Back when I was in high school, I won the Betty Crocker Homemaker of Tomorrow Award. The "trophy" was a pin, about two inches across, shaped like a heart, and with proper emblems and inscriptions on it.

I had kept it all these years, but seldom wore it. One Sunday morning, I decided to wear it because I thought it went well with my outfit of the day. I was pleased with the outcome until my teenage granddaughter said to me, "Mucho, did you get that out of the cereal box this morning?"

PINK FLAMINGOES

My husband has an absolute aversion to pink flamingoes—not to the birds themselves, but to the hot pink plastic ones that appear in the arid lawns of west Texas, those that dangle from the rear-view mirrors of a few vehicles, and those that appear on drinking glasses.

Knowing this "thing" Dick has about pink flamingoes, our longtime friends, the Baldwins, thought they had found a truly perfect gift for my husband. They purchased pink flamingo house shoes in his size, wrapped them, and waited for birthday time.

We were all gathered around celebrating, and it was time to open presents. With cameras poised to catch Dick's reaction, the fun began. Of course, he couldn't believe they even found such an item in a shoe store. He was required to try them on AND model the fine specimens. The shoes are fuzzy, bright pink, and feature a curved neck and large beak, not to mention popping eyes!

Dick has been known actually to wear these house shoes because they're warm in the wintertime. He also makes sure no one else is around but the two of us!

GETTING ROLES STRAIGHT

It was Saturday morning, and my husband and I were in no great hurry to get up. Our young children, three and four, had gotten up and were playing around. They had been downstairs to check on the status of breakfast, and of course, there was not any. They came back up to complain about it. I said to Andrew, "I thought you were going to make our breakfast today."

"You are the cooker; I am just the eater," was his reply.

Daddy and the Churning Duties

Our milk cows at the ranch were good producers, which meant we had a good bit of milk, cream, and butter. In the distribution of job assignments, it became my daddy's job to do the churning. Mother worked the milk out of the freshly churned butter, molded it in the little wooden box designed for such, then wrapped it in the proper paper so it could be stored to be eaten as needed.

Daddy had done the churning when he was young using an old dasher-type churn. He was not keen on this method! The hand-cranked Daisy churns were not his favorite either.

So, what was the answer?

He decided he would have to invent a workable churn that would get the job done and not be too labor intensive. His first idea was to use the hand-held garden tractor (gasoline operated) as his power source. Now, for a container: he found a square metal box about eight inches on a side, with a volume of about two gallons. It even had a fitting lid on it! He couldn't just sit it on the ground, and if he put it on the garden tractor, it would vibrate off and fall on the ground with cream running everywhere. So, he built a sturdy platform with a support rack to hold his metal container.

At this point, he had a suitable cream holder and had developed a paddle to fit in it that would move around and turn that cream into butter. He now had Part A and Part B and needed to connect them. After several tries, he designed a belt that got the power applied to the churn, and it worked! Over the next several years, Daddy turned out lots of pounds of butter, and he was very, very proud of his "invention."

Hot Cake Hospitality

Mrs. Boyd was a dapper, older widow who lived in Balmorhea. She had no family who lived nearby, so about every Sunday after church, she would ask my mother to "eat out" with her. My mother's answer was always the same: "Mrs. Boyd, I can't. Duncan and the cowboys are waiting on me right now at the ranch to get home and put their dinner on the table."

Then, one Sunday morning, Daddy said to mother, "Momma, I am going to take Pete and go to Toyah to help Sonny McElroy, so you can 'eat out' with Mrs. Boyd today!"

Well, lo and behold, Mrs. Boyd did not make it to church that Sunday. Mother thought she would go home, have a quiet lunch, and watch some basketball games on the t.v.

She drove around to the back of the ranch house, started to get out of the car, and met a little girl right at the back door. Mother said hello and then asked her if her name was Lopez. Daddy had asked a Mr. Lopez to come to the ranch and butcher a hog. The little girl said, "No, my name is Brown, and my mother and daddy are sitting on the front porch."

Before Mother could even get into the house, the parents met her at the back door. Mother invited them in, then excused herself to change out of her church clothes before she came back to the kitchen and began preparing everyone something to eat.

As she had not even expected to be home at noon, she had not prepared any lunch, much less a Sunday dinner. But, being the hospitality minded sort she is, mother set about to prepare something! After the three guests assured her that they did like bacon and hot cakes, she made that, and they sat down to eat.

About two bites into the meal, a big teenage boy burst into the kitchen. Without saying "hello" or anything, he walked over to the table and checked out what was being eaten by the others. The man introduced the boy as their son. A place at the table was set for him, and mother served up some more pancakes and bacon. Once he was into eating, he said, "My uncle and aunt are still hunting rocks, but they will be here soon."

No sooner said than done, so another round of hot cakes and bacon for the two of them.

The man then said to Mother, "We understand that you ALWAYS made a big lunch on Sundays so we didn't bother to call."

My mother replied that that was normally true—just NOT this Sunday!

While they kept on eating, one of Daddy's friends from Pecos came to put the butchered hog in the freezer so he could come back later and cut it up. Since he was in a hurry, he declined the offer to come in and have some hot cakes and bacon.

With a break in the action, mother got busy cleaning up the dishes and utensils. Two young men from town came in the back door. They wanted to go horseback riding. They were informed that the men were away and if they wanted to ride, they could go saddle the horses themselves. This was agreeable to the two young men, but they mentioned that they had not had lunch and that it smelled wonderful in the kitchen. You gotta know—Mother fixed them some hot cakes and bacon!

By looking at the clock, Mother knew she wasn't going to see any basketball that afternoon. So, once again she dug into cleaning up the kitchen. OOPS! More traffic inbound—it was Daddy's friend who had been there earlier, but had not eaten. Only this trip to the ranch, he had brought his wife and sister with him, and none of the three of them had eaten supper. Trying to be cheerful, my mother asked, "How would you like some hot cakes and bacon?"

They agreed that that would be a real treat. Once again, Momma made up more hot cake batter and fried some bacon.

Thinking her rather long day was finally finished, she looked up just in time to see Daddy coming in. He said, "Momma, we had a real nice lunch, but that was seven hours ago."

Therefore, as the rule of the day had been, Daddy and Pete had some hot cakes and what was left of the bacon. (I'm not certain Momma ever got around to eating supper.)

Daddy cleaned up and went on to bed. In a few minutes, Mother actually did complete the kitchen cleanup. Then she, too, prepared for bed. As she was crawling in for some well-deserved rest, Daddy said, "Hey Momma, how was your lunch with Mrs. Boyd?"